EVEN GREATER OPERATIC DISASTERS

Disaster Prize! See page twenty

EVEN GREATER
OPERATIC DISASTERS

HUGH VICKERS

Illustrated by Michael ffolkes

Jill Norman & Hobhouse

First published 1982 by
JILL NORMAN & HOBHOUSE LTD
90 Great Russell Street, London WC1B 3PY

Text © Hugh Vickers 1982
Illustrations © Michael ffolkes 1982

ISBN 0 906908 62 0

Printed in Great Britain by
BUTLER & TANNER LTD
Frome and London

For Silvio Varviso

CONTENTS

I am grateful to the following opera fanatics who have helped in various ways: Anthony Besch, Sir Ashley Clarke, William Foster, Gert Frobe, John Kirkwood, Caroline McCullough, Patricia Moynagh, Charles Osborne, Marita Prantner, Peter Ustinov, Silvio Varviso, Judy Woodhouse, Ilsa Yardley; also to Gaynor Johnson, who typed the book and contributed a disaster of her own.

Finally, I am especially delighted to have contributed one of the first titles to appear under the new publishing imprint of Jill Norman and Hobhouse Ltd and wish it a non-disastrous and lucrative (for all of us) future.

HUGH VICKERS

Publisher's note

As in the previous volume, some of the events in this book are well documented and incontrovertibly true; others have a basis in truth but have been somewhat embellished along the way; still others are almost certainly apocryphal, but '*se non è vero, è ben trovato*'. And, once again, the author and publisher will be delighted to hear from members of the public and of the operatic trade about new disasters for future volumes.

INTRODUCTION

It is with some hesitation that I offer to my readers yet a further study of operatic disasters. I do so mainly in order to clear up the glaring omissions and scandalous inaccuracies which, alas, characterised my former volume; correspondents from all over the world have reproached me for these errors, but the most thunderous attack has come from California. Miss Linda Latz of San Francisco, for instance, writes 'How could you say that Lily Pons ever performed Santuzza - or are you suggesting that I have missed a San Francisco *Cavalleria Rusticana* in thirty-six years?'

Far more grave, however, is my shocking lack of reference to many parts of the world in which operatic disasters, formerly a tiny sapling, have become a mighty tree. Here Australia leads the field. I can only apologise to my many friends and correspondents down under for my hitherto abject lack of reference to their stupendous contribution to this subject.

April, 1981   HUGH VICKERS

GENERAL MAYHEM

Thank you Mrs Jenny Hill for this transcendental story – raising Australia at a stroke to the level of London, San Francisco, nay, even New York, as a forum for great operatic disasters.

Salome
Richard Strauss,
Perth, Western
Australia,
1978

The somewhat staid through fair city of Perth hardly seems a likely choice for a production of *Salome*, but the young iconoclastic producer was determined to give the people of Perth the shock of their lives with this rich orgy of German incest, necrophilia and doom. He instructed the property department to make an exceptionally gory and revolting head of John the Baptist to be brought on at the end for the great final scene where Salome insists on kissing his mouth. As rehearsals wore on, however, the usual rift on the matter of good taste developed between the producer and the director of the theatre board. After endless arguments the producer was persuaded to the point of allowing the head to be brought in covered with a white cloth. However, by this time the soprano, an imported East German lady of 'commanding and awesome stature', had fallen out with the stage-hands, with the result that when the first night came, the audience stayed transfixed until the final scene, all concerned looking on with agonised apprehension as the silver platter bearing the Baptist's head was slowly carried on. 'Daughter of Herodias, you blaspheme', cried Herod. 'I care not, I will kiss his mouth' Salome replied. The head got nearer, the orchestra lashed itself up yet again into a necrophiliac, erotic frenzy, the moment came, she snatched away the cloth . . . and on the charger was a pile of ham sandwiches.

She collapsed in a heap of laughter and the curtain was rung down.

Tosca
Teatro Colón,
Buenos Aires,
c. *1950*

More *Tosca* horrors – Maria Jeritza tripped up and fell flat on her face in front of Scarpia. No time to get up, so she nobly sang the whole of '*Vissi d'arte*' lying on her stomach. Quite possible – it is often done lying down, but usually on a *chaise longue*, lying or bending backwards over Scarpia's table, or some other inconvenient position. The trouble was that the Colón stage is vast and there simply was not any light at the place she was lying – by the time the wandering follow-spots had got her in their searchlight beam she had finished.

From South America where to go but Ireland? But of course producing opera in Ireland other than at the delicious Wexford Festival is fraught with absurd problems and even Wexford, as we shall see, can contribute its disaster. I remember Anthony Besch telling me about working with the Dublin Grand Opera Society years ago; he said that one would arrive having been given, say, forty-eight hours' rehearsal time, to prepare five or six operas; the singers straggling in from various remote areas, absolutely no stagehands available: apparently those in command, if asked where a given person was, would invariably give that enchanting/infuriating Irish reply, 'Och, he went to the West'. The result was that the entire stage crew used to be made up of Anthony's grand Irish friends – one would find Jonathan and Desmond Guinness humping enormous pieces of scenery, the Earl of Rosse perched in the flies scattering the artificial snow in *La Bohème*. . . . However the other peril was of course the audience: it was not lacking – it was passionate, enthusiastic, almost Italian in the frequency of its interjections, for instance 'What the devil's all this about then?' at the moment of Leporello's escape in *Don Giovanni*, Act II.

However, this I particularly like –

La Bohème
Giacomo Puccini,
Dublin Grand
Opera
Society

The tenor was not merely drunk, but absolutely paralytic. When he was searching on the floor for Mimi's key he bumped into her head so hard that she gave an audible cry of pain: the start of '*Che gelida manina*' was delayed because he literally could not find her hand (admittedly the lighting was not very good); a guffaw went round the house when he finally accepted the invitation to go into the Café Momus – it was obvious that he would be barely able to make it, but he did manage to stagger off on his top C before collapsing in the wings.

The interval was particularly long, with a sweepstake developing among the public as to whether he would reappear or not, and if not, what conceivable excuse would be given; but in fine Irish style the management produced something more totally unexpected than anyone would have thought possible. The usual sheepish figure in a dinner-jacket appeared in front of the curtain and explained that the unfortunate tenor had just returned from a trip to West Africa and was suffering from a slight case of malaria. To which a voice from the gods replied, 'I wish I had a bottle of that, then . . .'.

While on the subject of problems arising from the staging of '*Che gelida manina*' we surely ought not to forget Caruso.

La Bohème
New York,
The Metropolitan
Opera,
1936

As is well known, Caruso did not like Nellie Melba – to such a point indeed that, on one occasion, just before he announced her tiny hand was frozen, he grabbed from the wings and placed in it a hot potato. But is this wholly correct? By some accounts it was, even more offensively, a sausage. I trust my readers will devote their considerable scholarship to resolving the precise truth about this incident. For example, Melba's reaction is not recorded: a bottle of champagne for the reader who can devise the most ingenious solution on averted disaster lines. After all, here is this impoverished seamstress in Paris, in the middle of winter; clearly the gift of a hot potato from a complete stranger might be the most exquisite her heart could desire: should she for instance not clutch it fervently to her lips rather than hitting him in the face with it.... Ah well, I leave it to you.

I used to think of French opera audiences as being exclusively on the bourgeois, I-am-there-to-be-seen side. But the dynamic growth of new festivals in France – at Albi for instance – utterly belies this. Research in England shows rather that it is here that the classic audience attitudes die hardest.

Der Rosen-kavalier
Glyndebourne
Festival,
1980

This splendid production was designed by the great Erté, who decided, like Visconti, to up-date the work, in this case into the mid-nineteenth century rather than the world of Art Nouveau. (I myself still cannot see why if *Capriccio* works in an eighteenth-century setting *Rosenkavalier* should not.) Nonetheless Erté's costumes were fabulous, a riot of Second Empire style and colour. This I think gives special point to a conversation over-heard in the interval:

MAN TO WOMAN: 'Do you know who wrote it?'
WOMAN TO MAN: 'I think it must be Mozart.'
MAN TO WOMAN: 'Why Mozart?'
WOMAN TO MAN: 'Oh you know, because of the costumes.'

Otello
Giuseppe Verdi,
Royal Opera
House, Covent
Garden,
1960s

One of the dottiest of overheard remarks was collected by the publisher of this book at Covent Garden. Mario del Monaco was unable to sing *Otello* and at short notice the hitherto little known Canadian tenor James McCracken was brought in. It was a debut to match Sutherland's as Lucia a few years before; the entire cast, including Tito Gobbi as Iago, sang like angels and McCracken was, as everyone now knows, a revelation in the title part. As the audience, drained of emotion and exhausted by clapping, left the stalls, one dowager said disapprovingly to another 'My dear, I always knew mixed marriages were a mistake, and that simply *proved* it.'

Covent Garden audiences appear however to have livened up considerably recently, doubtless due to the harsh strictures in my previous book. For example, during the final performance of *Norma* in which Sylvia Sass made a clearly somewhat controversial appearance in the title role, a splendid claque-against-claque fight broke out, using rolled-up copies of *The Times*, umbrellas, parliamentary order papers, indeed anything that came to hand. The production was indeed slightly ill-fated –

Norma
Vincenzo Bellini,
Royal Opera
House,
Covent Garden,
1979

Shirley Verrett revealed that gongs can be as bad as anvils. The gong was a gigantic J. Arthur Rank affair (it had to be, since a stagehands' walk-out had eliminated most of the rest of the set). At the climactic moment in Act II Miss Verrett took the first of her three swipes which would summon the Druids to her side, with such force that the head of the gong stick shot across the stage, where it lay until expertly back-heeled into the wings by a member of the chorus. Poor Miss Verrett, she now had to hit the gong twice more with the bare stick, with the Covent Garden audience in hysterics. At least she did not hit anyone - the nineteenth-century German soprano, Therese Tietjens took such a back swing before striking that she hit the tenor on the nose, laying him out cold. I will add that Bellini had truly bad luck with the use of that gong. How *can* we of the post-Victorian world ever fail to associate it with *Upstairs, Downstairs*? Instead of a priestess calling her people to the sacred fight for liberty, she suggests rather a parlour-maid deputising for the butler in summoning a tiresomely elderly house-party to dinner.

A Covent Garden audience reaction I have recently heard, however, is a splendid one my late friend Philip Hope-Wallace told:

La Traviata
Giuseppe Verdi,
Royal Opera
House,
Covent Garden,
mid-1970s

In the middle of a magnificent performance by Ileana Cotrubas with Alfredo Kraus in the love duet, the curtain was rung down because of a bomb scare. (It was one of those bomb seasons – the conductor, Silvio Varviso, narrowly escaped from a bomb thrown into Scott's restaurant.) Anyway, Philip, who was not to be deterred from opera pleasures by such minor matters, commented afterwards, 'Why didn't John Tooley [the General Administrator] take a more robust view? It was a twenty-minute warning and we were only twelve minutes from the end of the scene.' I fear however that Cotrubas and Kraus would probably have thought that their love, already difficult enough, had become simply too fraught in such circumstances. . . .

I should add that nothing on earth has ever been known to scare Mme Cotrubas; her first night as Violetta in *La Traviata* at La Scala was a classic case of averted disaster. It took place before the London incident described above; she was very young and though she knew the role of Violetta, she had never before performed it in public. La Scala were opening the season with a Luchino Visconti *Traviata*, scheduled for a Monday, but both Maria Callas and her understudy fell ill on the preceding Friday; unable to cast from within Italy they telephoned Mme Cotrubas's house near Glyndebourne, but she was shopping in London and her husband was in the bath so he missed the call. When eventually they did get through, he packed their suitcases, put in the *Traviata* score and dashed to London. They arrived at Heathrow just in time for the last plane to Milan, but the airport was fogbound and the flight cancelled. Next morning, Saturday, all flights out of Heathrow were cancelled, and the fog deepened. They stayed at a hotel near the airport. Sunday dawned, Heathrow was clear but Milan–Linate completely fogbound. Monday, the day of the performance, both airports were clear and they arrived in Milan to find a motorcade with police escort headed by the Mayor of Milan, Ghiringelli, the director of La Scala, and a somewhat tense Visconti. They dashed through the specially cleared streets, got through one rehearsal of the more difficult passages of the work; Mme Cotrubas changed into her costume, went on without a moment's rest and received twenty-four curtain calls.

There are, of course, disasters caused by simple absenteeism, frequently due to the proximity to the stage-door of a public house, or some other form of hostelry. Berlioz in his *Memoires* points out that it was rare indeed for half the Paris Opera orchestra to be present simultaneously, but the chorus can be even worse. In Italy they have been known to demand extra money for the sort of opera – *The Magic Flute* for instance – which ends with a rousing chorus as opposed to the ideal, *Manon Lescaut*, say, where they can all go home after the third act. Nonetheless –

Manon Lescaut
Giacomo Puccini,
The Welsh
National
Opera,
Brighton
Festival,
1978

At the end of a triumphant last act the conductor found that not only the chorus but the entire orchestra had fled, leaving nobody but Manon and Des Grieux on stage. He was in the embarrassing position of profusely thanking a completely empty orchestra pit. Perhaps after a hard stint in Cardiff the legendary attractions of Brighton were just too much, or maybe the Welsh players had heard something about Brighton's opening and closing hours.

**La Sonnam-
bula**

*Vincenzo Bellini,
La Scala,
Milan,
1963*

Bellini's *La Sonnambula* provides surely the hardest possible test of the relationship between singer and orchestra. To somnambulate effectively you have obviously got to have your eyes shut - so no chance of even a modicum of visual help from prompter or conductor. I have always wondered how Callas performed the part with such utter conviction, as at La Scala in 1963.

In 1966 I had the opportunity to ask Luchino Visconti how he had arranged this scene to such great effect. The answer turned out to be that he had made brilliant use of a sense one does not normally associate with the operatic stage - the sense of smell. Visconti invariably wore a handkerchief in his top pocket with a touch of an English fragrance he was fond of. When Callas said she liked it too, it occurred to Visconti to place one of his handkerchiefs on the bed during the sleep-walking scene so that Callas would be guided towards it by the scent alone. This worked perfectly night after night. Only later did it occur to him that it was fortunate indeed that no member of the Scala orchestra - or audience - was wearing that particular scent - otherwise we would have had another, and truly catastrophic opera disaster.

Anna Bolena
Gaetano Doni-
zetti,
La Scala,
Milan,
1961

More homage to Callas. Rarely in operatic history has a singer brought the theatre and real life together with such tremendous effect as when the diva, on her way to execution as Anne Boleyn, looked straight up at the empty box of her enemy the theatre director Ghiringhelli exactly on the words '*Il palco funesto*' (*palco* in Italian happens by a weird coincidence to mean both execution block and opera box).

Carmen
Los Angeles

Important news from Los Angeles. The reader may recall how in my last volume we described an unfortunate Italian tenor in Mexico City who during an interval in a production of *Carmen* was arrested in a nearby bar by the local police because he looked like Don José – i.e. a military deserter. It now appears that performing *Carmen* can be dangerous even for members of the orchestra. The trumpeter Gilbert Johns of the Los Angeles Philharmonic was standing in the woods surrounding the Hollywood Bowl about to give the off-stage trumpet call which summons Don José back to barracks. A tidy-minded policeman arrested him on the grounds that to be standing in the Robin Hood Dell dressed in a white summer suit holding a trumpet amounted at the least to highly suspicious behaviour. Poor Mr Johns seems to have had more than his fair share of bad luck in open-air events. He was for instance once attacked by a swarm of bees in the middle of Bruckner's second symphony....

Don Giovanni
W. A. Mozart

Perhaps all music is really an assault on our emotions, even Mozart. The recent film of *Don Giovanni* by Joseph Losey is a very good case in point. At the risk of digressing from my already highly digressive theme, what actually does happen in *Don Giovanni*? This seems an excellent place to argue the question of what precisely has occurred at the beginning of the opera. If Giovanni has in fact seduced Donna Anna, her great Act I aria in which she describes the event to Ottavio is a lie. It also appears to stretch the rules of dramatic probability to an absurd extent in that the opera, though called '*dramma giocoso*' by the librettist Da Ponte, is founded in the *opera buffa* tradition and is therefore basically realistic. On the other hand, everyone feels the erotic content in Donna Anna's words '*Era già alquanto avanzata la notte ...*' My own feeling is that in eighteenth-century opera, as in all other classical works of art, one should assume that it means what it says unless there is some evident reason to the contrary. If Anna means what she says, we have a much more coherent explanation than if she was in fact seduced by Giovanni. I think what we are hearing is the lament of a woman who was not seduced by him, but wishes she had been. Surely this is the first rebuff that Don Giovanni has ever received and it initiates the dramatic action and Giovanni's downfall. What Anna is clearly thinking is that her conventional morality (shown in the choice of Ottavio as her fiancé) and her stupid pride caused the death of her father. If this is not so, *why* does she say to Ottavio that she at first mistook Don Giovanni for him? If Ottavio had never visited and made love to Anna at night it would make no sense to say this to him. Clearly she did think it was Ottavio and

31

then found it was an unknown but extremely attractive man. She cried out – just as she says – and Giovanni made good his escape in order to avoid having to fight his way out through a whole pack of the Commendatore's men-at-arms. Otherwise, he would surely have stayed till early morning and then slipped out.

Some allusion must be made to Mr Jeremy Maddon-Simpson's astonishing theory that in the course of the opera Don Giovanni clearly seduces six women. This is rather startling when we compare it with traditional criticisms, such as that of Edward J. Dent (in *Mozart's Operas*) who holds that Giovanni is a complete paper tiger who seduces no one at all. What a classic example of the ambiguity of opera that two such diverse views could be held. Challenged to defend his position, he presented the following Leporello-like list:

1. Donna Anna, at the beginning.
2. Zerlina, in the first act finale when she screams off stage (he would have had to have been very quick about it, but I suppose an expert like Giovanni would just about have had time).
3. Donna Elvira's servant girl, after the serenade, on the assumption that no woman could possibly resist being sung to like that. (I like this theory because there always seems something curious about the immediate switch of emphasis after the serenade away from Don Giovanni on to the escaping Leporello.)
4–5. Two village girls in the interval but before the opening of Act 2. 'If Giovanni was fleeing from the vice squad at the end of Act I, why is he so cheerful when Act II begins?' This point was well taken by Losey in his film –

IL
COMMENDATORE

he sets the Act II opening duet with Giovanni
disporting himself with a half-naked village
girl.

6. Leporello's wife. This I like very much
because people in classical opera mean what
they say. Not only does Don Giovanni say
to Leporello that he ran into a lady who
knew him, but when Leporello says 'and
suppose it was my wife?' Giovanni roars with
laughter and says *'meglio ancora!'*, thus trig-
gering the statue's first pronouncement *'di
rider finirai. . . .'* and thus the dénouement of
the opera. Giovanni is blatantly teasing Leporello about an affair he's been having with
his wife, probably for some time (it would
be absolutely in character and would explain
a lot about the curious attachment between
Giovanni and Leporello).

As indicated, I only take complete exception to
No 1 on this list, partly because I think it would
spoil the effect of the work if Elvira and Anna
were both women in exactly the same position.
They would, in fact, given the conventions of
eighteenth-century opera, be deadly rivals. But
they are not – they have the utmost sympathy for
each other, though their attitudes to Don Giovanni
are opposed. Anna wants vengeance, but the feeling is tempered by remorse for the death of her
father; Elvira is prepared to the very last moment
to love Don Giovanni and to forgive him. For this
reason the words in her final recitative, *'aperto
veggio il baratro mortal'* was absolutely rightly inter-
preted by Losey as a religious confession in which
she pleads for his soul and her own. Her last words
are effectively *'mi tradi quell' Alma ingrata'*, while

Big-bang theory

Reading CSO percussionist Patricia Dash's comment ["Heavy Metal," Oct.31 that playing the cymbal can be a mix of "99 percent patience and 1 percent terror" reminded me of the moment of truth told of another cymbal player in the 1930s.

A friend who had played at that time in a symphony orchestra in Syracuse, N.Y., related to me that their cymbal player frequently lost his place and accordingly often struck his cymbals at most inappropriate times. At the final rehearsal before an important concert, the conductor warned him that he would be fired if he missed a critical cymbal crash during their concert performance. This was a threat to be taken seriously in the depths of the Depression.

The cymbal player correctly counted the empty measures before his moment of glory. He struck his cymbals, one of which hung on a stand before him, with such force that the hanging cymbal came loose from its stand, sailed through the air, and landed on its edge on the stage before the orchestra. It then rolled around in smaller and smaller circles, finally coming to rest with a final clatter.

The orchestra attempted to carry on to the end of the score, but it was too much, and one by one they laid down their instruments and joined in the hysterical laughter of the audience. The unfortunate percussionist took his music from his stand, left the stage and was never seen again.

Howard Kittel
Naperville

Anna's, be it noted, are addressed to Ottavio *'non mi dir, bell'idol mio, che son io crudel con te.'*

So there we are back where we started. She *does* love Ottavio, and he did come regularly to visit her at night. So there, dear reader, that's my theory – you can disagree with it all you like but I won't budge an inch.

Even Greater Operatic Disasters

This discussion of *Don Giovanni* and especially
Joseph Losey's film of it, reminds us that we must
refer to –

Boris Godunov
*Modest Mus-
sorgski,
Paris Opéra,
1980*

As with the *Don Giovanni*, most of the conventional opera critics found this one 'delightful,
but infuriating'. This was because Losey decided
to turn the most basic of all operatic conventions
upside down by having the singers in front and the
orchestra playing in a sort of gigantic Russian
snow hat behind them. Result – the singers
sounded as close up as in, say, one of those garish
Decca Wagner recordings, while the orchestra
sounded as if they were playing in the next room,
or possibly even a few streets away. No marks here
for Losey, though full marks to that superb baritone Ruggiero Raimondi for an epic Boris.

Having returned to France, we certainly ought
to mention what happened at the first known
performance in France of one of Sir Thomas
Beecham's favourite operas.

Le Tableau
Parlant
André Grétry,
Lyon, 1936

This is a frothy *opéra bouffe* by the admirable Italian-trained Grétry, who is in fact Belgium's only important composer. (The reader will, I hope recall the Avenue Grétry leading to the Grande Place in Brussels, and, far more important, the superb Restaurant Grétry therein.) The plot is pure *commedia dell'arte* – nasty old Cassandre is in love with his ward Isabelle, who is in love with handsome, young Léandre. Piero and Colombine (Isabell's confidante) make up the cast of five. About half-way through, Cassandre manages to get into his thick head that there is some kind of hanky-panky going on between all the other characters. He therefore pretends to leave for Paris, but in fact stays skulking round the house, to find out what is going on. Now, the stage is dominated by a giant life-size portrait of Cassandre. At the crucial moment of a love duet between Isabelle and Léandre, Cassandre achieves the ultimate in voyeurism by cutting out the face of the portrait and substituting his own face looking through. (I know this sounds a bit much even for opera but I have seen a production and it is quite hilarious.) So it would have been at Lyon, except that the pre-cut face refused to come out and the singer was so annoyed that when he got behind it he slipped and the whole thing – man, picture, face, the lot – came crashing to the ground. I think the reason was that to get to the face height he had to stand on a table – fatal.

Carmen
Georges Bizet,
Bologna, 1958

In the Lilas Pastia act both Don José and Escamillo fell off two separate tables, José's case at the end of his flower aria. What a dope – no wonder Carmen turns him down. As a matter of fact I have always thought that the recruitment of Don José suggests disturbing thoughts about the military standards of the Spanish army – one can hardly imagine him leading an effective *coup* for instance. Similarly, in Escamillo's case one wonders how a man incapable of standing on a table for three minutes without falling over would have much chance in the bull ring.

Anyway, with tables the problem is not how you get on the thing, but how on earth you get off it. If you step off it via a chair or bench (*Carmen*, Palermo 1981) it looks hopelessly weak. The only thing is to jump off it but then you must have some goal, aim or objective, preferably someone's arms.

Così Fan Tutte
W. A. Mozart,
Venice, 1974

This beautiful production, originally by Günther Rennert, had some splendid table-jumping in the first scene. Rennert very sensibly sets this in an inn (I cannot think why this is not always done – where else would one find three men making sordid bets) and there are therefore plenty of tables. Fernando jumped on one to deliver '*una bella serenata*' and Guglielmo onto another for '*in onor di Citerea*'. Here they looked perfectly natural with Alfonso on the ground between them. When he said '*saro anche io tra i convitati*' they both jump down simultaneously, and the three men immediately take hands to swear the oath. It was all highly effective.

Writing this here in Florence I am reminded of an event which was not an operatic disaster exactly, but a true operatic tragedy –

Egmont
Goethe/Ludwig
van Beethoven,
Palazzo Pitti,
Florence, 1967

'But it is not an opera' the reader is crying. Well to be precise it is a 'melodrama', but when you hear the whole work with all six pieces of the Beethoven incidental music (not just the famous overture) and when these are played by a large symphony orchestra in front of the stage conducted by Gianandrea Gavazzeni and the epic staging is by Visconti, we surely have more opera than anything else.

As the rehearsals went on, the text and music became even more fully integrated. During the Beethoven pieces – some of considerable length – the actors would freeze, forming a tableau superbly expressive of the emotional point reached (e.g. as when Egmont hands the Spanish Governor his sword). The dress rehearsal came – open air in the Pitti Palace courtyard on a perfect June evening. The fabulous setting and costumes – the light glinting on the breastplates of the Spanish guards – suggested now a Rembrandt, now a Velazquez come to life. I had the pleasure of watching this sitting next to Marcello Mastroianni – we were both riveted, hypnotised. Next evening, the opening – half an hour before the start the heavens opened and it rained as only Florence knows how. And believe it or not, it did so with absolute regularity for the scheduled week of the performances. The general public never saw it once and it was never repeated. Poor Visconti – but even the greatest are at the mercy of wind and weather. His film team for *Death In Venice* was kept idle for fifteen days because the cameraman was unhappy about the light for one single shot. . . .

Carmen
Heidelberg The conductor Ian Reid, recalls 'When I conducted *Carmen* in Heidelberg, Don José dis-
covered too late that he had forgotten to bring the
knife on stage to stab Carmen in the last scene. He
decided to strangle her instead. The girl playing
Carmen thought he had gone insane and fought
back like a tigress. Somehow, she managed to go
on singing throughout a prolonged and somewhat
muted strangulation.'

Albert
Einstein While this is not precisely an operatic disaster
it would seem to exhibit the quality we
have found in them – perhaps in a supreme form.
The great Albert Einstein was among other things
a brilliant amateur violinist – he led a very fine
amateur/quasi-professional quartet at Harvard for
many years. One evening he simply couldn't get
it right. (What violinist doesn't know the feeling.)
It was, of course, one of those 'easy' early Haydn
quartets. After Einstein failed to get the second
movement started correctly for the fourth time,
the cellist looked up at him in despair and said 'The
problem with you, Albert, is that you simply can't
count.'

La Bohème
London Opera
Centre

The soprano Linda Esther Gray recalls that 'I was the very last student to be trained at the old Opera Centre in the East End of London. The only time I've ever seen a singer fall asleep on stage was in an Opera Centre production.

'The poor tenor in *La Bohème* was unwell and had filled himself up to the eye balls with Valium. I was playing Mimi and was dying in Act IV. Musetta produced an expensive muff to keep me warm on my deathbed and I asked if she had bought it. The tenor was supposed to sing 'I did' but as he (apparently sunk in despair over the foot of the bed) was sound asleep, Musetta sang the line instead of him That's what I call presence of mind'.

Thea Musgrave
London Opera Centre, 1961

I was assisting that most meticulous of directors, Anthony Besch, in one of the first performances of this excellent work, conducted by the composer. The plot revolves almost entirely around the presence of a corpse in bed – he has just died before the opera begins – and concerns the reactions of his family and friends. Therefore it is of paramount importance that there should actually *be* a corpse in the bed. The props department had made a really excellent and realistic dummy. Anthony, quite rightly, trusted neither me nor anyone else to make certain that all was ready, and insisted on carrying the corpse on himself. However, in the flurry that precedes any opera performance, he forgot until the very last moment, and the curtain rose to reveal to the astonished audience an elegantly dinner-jacketed figure rushing across the stage clutching a very life-like body. After the intensely grim and funereal overture it did not strike quite the right note, not least because the opera is set in medieval Scotland.

Don Carlo
G. Verdi,
Royal Opera
House,
Covent Garden,
London, 1959

One of the most attractive and eye-catching features of this Visconti production was a real tennis match which took place in the second act, behind the central characters in the palace of the Queen of Spain. On the first night, at which I was present, it was an elegant Velazquez-like scene, with two extras batting a small tennis ball to and fro very slowly, not interfering with the main action. On the second night, however, the duty fell to two Royal Opera extras whose spare-time passion was tennis. Completely forgetting where they were or what they were doing they started hitting the ball in real earnest. The match ended with a terrific forearm smash, which fortunately missed Boris Christoff, singing Philip II, by inches before landing in the orchestra pit.

Pelléas et Mélisande
Claude Debussy
(date and locale unknown)

Debussy's *Pelléas et Mélisande* is fraught with dangers. So much can go wrong and nowhere so easily as in the scene in which Mélisande lets her hair down through the window under which her lover is waiting. Logistics dictate that the tress must be an inplausible and usually ludicrous five or six feet long, and many opera enthusiasts treasure memories of the hair detaching itself at Pelléas' first impassioned grope, leaving him sheepishly holding a hank of yellowish nylon or tow with a suddenly shorn Mélisande looking furiously down at him. Elisabeth Söderström, however, once encountered a new and original hazard.

She was singing Mélisande and had been provided with a hideously ugly reddish-blonde plait, six feet long, which she duly lowered out of the window.

Unfortunately, the end of the plait landed straight in Pelléas's open mouth and his singing died away in a strangled gurgle. Relations after that were distinctly chilly, though he did his best to embrace her with the enthusiasm the part demanded.

Le Nozze di Figaro
W. A. Mozart

Many a Count in *Le Nozze di Figaro* has found himself in most peculiar difficulties, greater even than those he has managed to create for himself. On one reported occasion he found that, owing to the fact that he had furnished the nuptial apartment for Figaro and Susanna particularly generously, the whole first act stage was cluttered with pieces of furniture covered with dust sheets. It so happened that this Count was a stand-in who had had little or no rehearsal before the production began. He therefore suddenly realised that when it came to the moment where he discovers Cherubino in hiding he had completely forgotten where to look. He rushed around, pulling sheet after sheet off piles and piles of furniture. Despite surreptitious and increasingly frantic attempts by Susanna and Basilio to point him in the right direction he became so baffled that the only way the opera could proceed was for Cherubino voluntarily to jump out of hiding, thus giving a very strong reverse twist to the plot.

Der Freischütz
Carl Maria von
Weber,
Hanover, 1960

I am most deeply grateful to Sir Ashley Clarke, former British Ambassador in Rome, and tireless organiser of Venice in Peril for the following story. Now with *Der Freischütz*, I hope the reader will agree, we enter the world of the absolutely incomprehensible. I have never met anybody who really knows what the opera is about. Silvio Varviso, despite having conducted the work many hundreds of times, tells me he doesn't know what it's about. August Everding, whose ravishing production was so much admired at Covent Garden three years ago, agrees that he too doesn't know what it is about. I certainly don't know. All I do know, or have ever gathered, is that the fatal seventh shot is not intended to hit Agathe - or rather it is, but it gets deflected on to Kaspar, which seems quite a good thing. Now, Sir Ashley assures me that on this particular occasion, however, it missed both of these characters and hit the tree, and that the stage hands, who didn't like that particular Max, dropped a dead hare out of the tree onto the stage. Poor shooting, if I may say so. To hit a hare which happened to be sitting in a tree with your *seventh* shot would disgrace even the proverbial Irishman who shot an arrow at the sky - and missed.

WAGNERIAN PROBLEMS

The traditional Wagner section leads off this time with an invaluable contribution from the tenor Alberto Remedios who has made such a magnificent showing in the current Covent Garden Ring Cycle.

Siegfried
Manchester,
1976

Siegfried approaches with the usual trepidation the sleeping form of Brünnhilde, dreading that moment of potential comedy when he removes her breastplate and starts back with the words, '*Das ist kein Mann.*' His heroic bearing eliminated any possibility of audience titters at this point, but even his professionalism was strained to the limit when he saw beneath the breastplate a note – DO NOT DISTURB, EARLY MORNING TEA 7.30 A.M.'

Die Walküre
La Scala,
1959

In one of innumerable disasters depending on the fact that one of the principals is taller than the other, Siegfried (Wolfgang Windgassen), who was wearing built-up shoes, lost his balance after pulling out Nothung from the tree-trunk, and on the run-up to Sieglinde fell over backwards on the raked stage. Seeing him approaching at a tremendous speed, she simply opened her legs and he sailed through beneath, ending up near the orchestra pit, ten yards down stage. It must have been one of the great slides in Wagner – he was later described as a polar bear coming down a waterchute – as opposed to mere falls such as Hans Hotter's in Covent Garden in 1948, which caused Philip Hope-Wallace to wonder publicly, 'Need the stage be built up like the Mappin Terraces at the Zoo? Valkyries are not antelopes. . . .'

Lohengrin
New York,
The Metropolitan
Opera,
1937

This is yet another magnificent Melchior story. He was all set for the moment in Act III when the evil Telramund tricks him in the bridal chamber. Imagine his utter consternation when, on diving under the bed to seize his hidden sword he found that the incompetent stage management had forgotten to put it there. Bereft of weapons he therefore met the astonished Telramund with a short left to the jaw – it did the trick.

Wagnerian Problems

Lohengrin
The Paris
Opéra

Again in Act III, the tenor singing Lohengrin ran into trouble, but this time not because he had lost his sword, but because like our Irish tenor he was unfortunately suffering from malaria. Perhaps his identification with the part had therefore become too complete – he simply found that his Elsa was so ravishingly attractive that the third time she was foolish enough to break his commandment by asking him his name he mentally jumped straight to the end of the opera and replied in the most ringing tones, '*Dein ritter, ich bin Lohengrin bekannt*' ('I, your knight, am called Lohengrin'). Fortunately the swan operators were not expecting this cue or we might have had the shortest *Lohengrin* ever. . . .

Here it would appear that the *souffleur* (prompter) was taken by surprise. How could he imagine that Lohengrin would forget the most important moment in his entire role? On the other hand, it is the duty of the *souffleur* to assume the worst. In Italy his task is made yet more demanding by the fact that he is also expected to conduct. It is not commonly realised that the conductor in the orchestra pit is not normally visible to the singers, nor, due to the enormous noise they are making themselves, is the orchestra audible. Hence the proliferation of closed-circuit television sets in modern opera houses and the vast artistic importance of the *souffleur* in older ones. The problem however is that the *souffleur* may actively disagree with the conductor's tempi to the point of deliberately establishing a completely different speed for the singers to that which prevails in the orchestra pit. An example —

Carmen
Georges Bizet,
Palermo,
1981

The leader of the orchestra, Gottfried Schmidt of Cologne (affectionately known in Germany as Fritz the Violin), told me of the orchestra's success in beating the singers to the end of the second act quintet by a full five seconds. The sound suggested Bizet as reinterpreted by a rather wild disciple of Webern. Nor did Gottfried think that matters were likely to improve. 'Next time we shall beat them by ten seconds,' he said proudly. Unfortunately I didn't stay in Palermo long enough to find out if he was right. . . .

There certainly is a special art to producing *Tristan*. During the second act it is obviously essential that the two lovers be lying down. It is however, very difficult for them, if they are lying anywhere realistically near each other, to see the conductor. If, however, they are not lying near each other, the impact of the duet is, shall we say, somewhat diminished. My brother, D. V. H. Vickers, tells me that the first time he saw *Tristan* was in Germany and that they were *not* lying near each other. The lady singing Isolde appeared to be lying on a mattress; it was only when she got up that he realised, as he put it, that she *was* the mattress.

Tristan und Isolde Richard Wagner, La Fenice, Venice, 1981 | Venice is of course always associated with disaster of one form or another, but this particular *Tristan* seems to have attracted the worst that La Serenissima can offer. The set appeared to be made entirely of black plastic, but the remarkable point of interest in the production occurred when Isolde says 'Put out the fateful light', in the second act. By some electronic mistake, every light in the theatre and auditorium chose this precise moment to blaze out. Peter Maag, conducting, carried on with his usual professionalism despite gales of laughter from the audience.

Idomeneo
W. A. Mozart,
La Fenice,
Venice,
1981

I don't want to knock La Fenice – if there is a more beautiful theatre in the world I'd like to know of it – but it appears to be ill-fated when it comes to any form of experimental production. (I did once see there the worst production of a Shakespeare play which I have ever seen. It was *The Winter's Tale*, and it so happened that Ezra Pound was among the audience. Next day, I met him at a lunch party given in his honour and we asked him what he had thought of it. In his usual laconic way he looked up and said 'Ham and Beat', which I thought summed it up perfectly.) On this occasion we had an *Idomeneo*, again decorated in black plastic, but with an attempt being made to represent the sea. A posse of dancers had been recruited to represent mermaids, seals and what appeared to be whales, also a number of boy dancers were lying around apparently pretending to be waves. All these people were in some way linked together, suggesting that it would be exceedingly alarming (my informant tells me) if, as was perfectly possible, someone suddenly needed to leave the stage in a hurry for some pressing personal reason. A kind of conga of waves, mermaids, seals – and whales – would have to leave the stage and return.

ANIMAL AND OTHER NATURAL
HAZARDS

My correspondence suggests that animals on the opera stage are behaving just as badly as ever. At Verona last year, for instance, the elephants were as good as gold but this time the camels disgraced themselves, unfortunately just in the entrance where the *corps de ballet* were about to come on. But how could I have omitted the following Beecham story?

Carmen
Georges Bizet,
Royal Opera
House,
Covent Garden,
c. 1932

Half-way through the third act Sir Thomas became aware that a horse was present on stage, intended to add local colour to the smugglers' cave scene. It was in fact the same old cabhorse that Covent Garden always used to use as Grane in *Götterdämmerung*, beloved by audiences for its droll habit of munching the scenery. On this occasion, however, it suddenly turned its back on the proceedings with a decisive and dramatic gesture and performed the ultimate indiscretion. The music stopped, silence fell through the theatre and from the pit came the judgment of Sir Thomas:
'A critic, by God'.

Boris Godunov
Modest Mus-
sorgski,
The Bolshoi
Theatre,
Moscow,
1979

The Bolshoi's horse is always of exquisite mus- icality. A correspondent writes that he was hypnotised by the way in which, throughout the two arias in which the singer was actually mounted on it, it flicked its enormous ears in time to the music with the beatific smile of a Derby winner. During the applause it would paw the ground, but this was rather unfortunate since its vast hooves produced a cavernous booming sound from the stage boards, inappropriate to a location on the Russian steppes. . . .

Bears One of my correspondents writes to say how
much he enjoys frequenting pubs immediately opposite stage doors, rubbing shoulders
with Roman soldiers, Dukes of Mantua, bears and
so on. *Bears?* This really started me thinking – in
how many operas do *bears* appear? It reminded me
of a conversation I had with the producer Aldo
Piccinato, years ago, in which he could not remember in which opera he had used live lions. We
tried a process of elimination: *Figaro?* Surely not.
The Merry Widow? Hardly. (The answer was, of
course, Donizetti's *Poliuto*. See *Great Operatic Disasters*.) However, the only opera I know with a
singing bear in it is Renaldo da Capua's *La Zingara*
(1752). This is a delectable *opera buffa* about a gypsy
brother and sister who cheat an elderly merchant
by selling him a performing bear which is in fact
the brother in disguise. In producing this work I
learnt a great deal (*a*) about the use of bears on
stage, (*b*) about the temper of tenors forced to
rehearse in a heavy bear costume in a hundred-
degree heatwave, but, above all, (*c*) about the glo-
rious intricacies of hiring a bear costume. I arrived
at Theatre Zoo, Drury Lane (to whom all thanks),
armed with the measurements of the tenor and
asked if they had a bear costume. The assistant
looked at me pityingly. 'What type of bear?' he
asked. 'Well, how many types are there?' 'Well,
there is three, ain't there, smooth bear, rough bear,
and very rough bear.' 'Well,' I said, 'just for the
hell of it, let's try very rough bear.' 'What type of
head?' he asked. 'Head?' 'Yes, rigid headpiece or
furry face-mask?' 'Well, let's try furry face-mask.'
'Colour?' (By now I was prepared for anything.)
'Well, how many colours have you got?' 'Well,

there is black, dark brown, medium brown, light brown, beige, pink-pantomime and white.'

I ended up with a wonderful shaggy dark brown creature and an auspicious, if unusual start, to the career of the young tenor Adrian Martin (now of English National Opera North).

Florence It appears that the baritone Gratarollo was forced throughout the entire season into some form of absurd rivalry with a *seal* in the local zoo. The animal cried out in delirious joy whenever he hit a high note. This suggests that zoos and opera houses should not be placed close together. . . .

The story suggests, not for the first time, that all opera depends essentially on the physical effect of the voice, whether it be human, animal or even something between the two. . . . For centuries the most admired operatic voice was the castrato. It is an authenticated fact that many boy singers preferred to undergo the operation rather than lose their voices, in the full knowledge of everything this choice would entail. Perhaps some of the desperate modern passion for our singers - Callas, Sutherland - does try to resurrect a similar absolute belief in art - if you like the frightening intensity which made *Cavalleria Rusticana* and *I Pagliacci* eliminate all rivals on the stage, if you like that element in opera which can only be called aggressive, an assault on the emotions.

Eighteenth-century accounts constantly refer to formal competition between the great castrati and various instruments, of which surprisingly the trumpet was the most popular. Castrati like Farinelli (1705-1782) had amazing international careers rewarded by staggering sums of money - more like today's film stars than opera singers. Furthermore, they had a wonderful time with the ladies, offering as they did, reassurance in an age of few or no contraceptive techniques. Poor Farinelli had to pay dearly for the admiration he aroused, however. For twenty-five years he found himself more or less trapped in the Spanish Court, forced

to sing the same arias every night for months at a time to the moronic Philip V, who would then attempt to imitate him with dismal howlings. (Domenico Scarlatti had had to endure much the same thing a few years before – hence we have over 600 magnificent sonatas.) Charles III in Naples was another eighteenth-century monarch who enjoyed throwing his weight around. He would pelt his courtiers with cream buns from the royal box – they just had to grin and bear it. Only in the still-surviving habit of dressing up to go to the opera does some of the feeling of royal influence remain. I met an old lady in Canareggio in Venice who said that she loved opera and listened to it on the radio, but had never been to La Fenice opera house. 'Why not?' I asked. '*Ma signore, non ho i vestiti.*' (But sir, I haven't the clothes.) I tried to explain that these days you don't exactly have to have a tiara to get in. She shook her head sadly '*Ormai è troppo tardi*' (and now it is too late).

Rigoletto
Giuseppe Verdi,
Sadler's Wells
Theatre,
London, 1950

Bees can be dangerous, dogs and horses disastrous, but I am most grateful to Mrs C. A. Rogers for pointing out that *cats* can be just as bad. Rigoletto was about to throw into the river the sack containing, not, as he believes, the dead body of his enemy, but of his beloved daughter Gilda. As the singer approached the tragic climax the audience started laughing. He turned round to find that a kitten had wandered on to the stage and was clawing at the sack containing the 'dead' body – which was given surreptitious jerks as the claws sank in. The singer finally found a moment in which to boot the animal from the stage.

THE MALEVOLENCE OF INANIMATE
OBJECTS

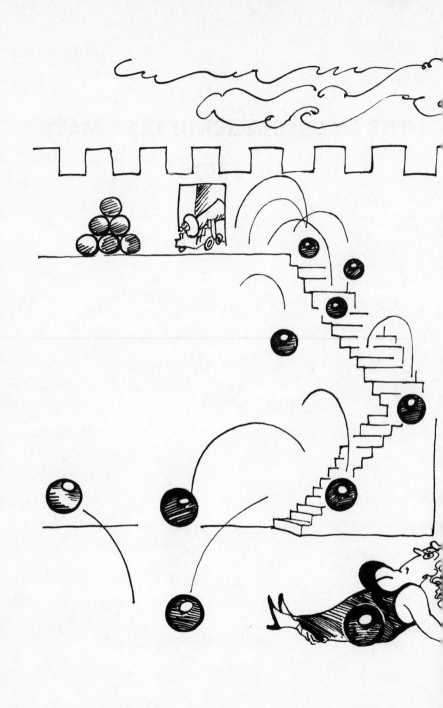

It was a cut-price production of this most accident-prone of operas, with minimal sets. At the last moment the producer sent a young assistant out to find some cannon balls to give verisimilitude to the final scene. The assistant, a youth of imagination and initiative, returned in the nick of time with a job lot of rubber beachballs. Hastily, they were painted black, equally hastily glued together to form a pile, and placed on the battlements, where they looked splendidly substantial. But, as Tosca rushed up the steps to take her fatal leap she managed to kick the pile. The glue must have been as cut-price as the beachballs, because the pile disintegrated and, liberated, the balls bounced down the steps, down the stage and soared over the orchestra pit to land in the stalls.

Over now to France, where again a thousand apologies to my French friends for failing to accord 'la belle France' the notoriety in this field of London or New York. One or two excuses – the first is that under the régime of M. Rolf Liebermann the Paris Opera has of course been transformed into one of the world's greatest houses; the second that almost all aspects of French opera which can be satirised have already been done by Berlioz in his memoirs. I can however proffer this from Mr Peter Ustinov –

Don Quixote
Jules Massenet,
The Paris
Opera

I quote his words, 'I had four windmills. The back one was working perfectly because it had a very small and therefore very intelligent man in it, thus this windmill was going around.... The next one had a much larger and much denser man and it was turning very much more slowly. The third one had two men in it who did not get on politically, so the thing was quite uncertain, and the one in front had an electric motor which suddenly, on the first night, went into reverse so the wind was blowing in a different direction....

The Magic Flute
W. A. Mozart,
English
National
Opera, 1977

One Saturday night the baritone Niall Murray was playing Papageno in the English National Opera production of *The Magic Flute*, sung, of course, in English. At once point, Papageno and Tamino are waiting for a chariot to descend from the flies containing the three boy spirits who will tell them where to go next.

'But the chariot got stuck somewhere above our heards out of sight and there was a distinct shortage of spirits, apart from the faint off-stage piping of distressed trebles.

' "I think I can hear a chariot", I sang hopefully. "Yes, so can I", echoed Tamino loudly into the wings. Stagehands were fighting somewhere in the void above us to untangle the chariot but without result.

'In opera, you sometimes have to judge the moment when the audience is about to laugh and get in before them. "No wonder it's late", I told them. "That chariot runs on British Rail standard gauge".

'In the end, the stage manager decided that he must at least deliver the contents of the chariot. The magic flute fell from aloft. There were supposed to be some bells but they never materialised. But a bowl of fruit did. It fell with a crash on my head and sent me reeling.'

Aida
Giuseppe Verdi,
Paris Opéra,
1971

Grace Bumbry, singing Amneris, was required to walk up an enormously impressive staircase – reminiscent of the order given by Robert de Montesquiou 'like the one in the Opera, only bigger' – when it slowly began to split down the middle into its two component parts, on each of which the singer had a foot. Only a balletic leap saved her from acute embarrassment, and indeed from being filleted like a kipper.

La Traviata
Giuseppe Verdi

The following story is told of Giuseppe di Stefano who was singing Alfredo. In the second act the libretto provides for him to hurl his card winnings at Violetta – symbol of payment for her past favours and the ultimate public insult. He reached into his breast pocket, then in gathering consternation into his trouser pockets and every other place where his dresser could have secreted the dummy notes. They were nowhere to be found, and he was forced to slap Violetta's face instead. She, quite unprepared for this assault, is said never to have forgiven him.

Moses and
Aaron
Arnold
Schoenberg,
Deutsch Oper
am Rheim,
Cologne,
1962

This production was already celebrated for Josef Greindl's performance as Moses. However on this particular night it ran into a problem. The orchestra was 'assisted' by a series of loudspeakers which both developed the orchestral sound and added a specially prepared stereophonic soundtrack. Unfortunately, by one of the laws we have begun to develop in opera disasters, the electronic system became inadvertently plugged in to the local U.S. Air Force base. Thus Moses found himself competing with a fantastic background of technical weather reports, snatches of Liberace and some of Elvis Presley's greatest hits.

It is true that Richard Strauss requires the tenor in *Intermezzo* to enter on skis – a treat all to infrequently offered to opera-goers, but at a recent Wexford Festival performance of Spontini's *La Vestale* the entire cast faced a kind of operatic Cresta Run.

La Vestale
Gasparo
Spontini,
Wexford
Festival,
1980

La Vestale is set in Imperial Rome, and for this Festival production the designer had reproduced the marble of the Roman Forum with flooring of shiny white plastic stretched over the steeply raked stage. The producer had considerately arranged for the plastic to be sprayed with a non-skid substance (the irreverent said it was lemonade), but on the final night it was forgotten. The tenor entered, top left, his feet shot from under him and he slid inartistically into the footlights. Struggling up, he managed to regain his feet and reach the comparative safety of the central altar, to which he clung, still singing. There he was joined by the High Priestess, who had managed to aim her skid more accurately. When the time came for the soprano – the Vestal of the title – to enter, she had been forewarned and stepped on exceedingly cautiously. She embarked on her big aria, and then realised that she was unable to move from the spot. Without stopping singing, she stepped into the wings, removed her shoes and returned. This had only made matters worse, and she vanished a second time, to re-appear without her tights. The superior adhesive qualities of bare feet triumphed and she was able to join the central group without loss of dignity. However, when the chorus – a crowd of priests, citizens and soldiers – entered, they had for some reason not taken in what was happening and one by one shot gloriously down the stage to join their colleagues in a struggling heap at the footlights.

***Die
Fledermaus***
*Johann Strauss
Deutsche Oper
am Rhein,
Cologne, 1962*

It was one of those glittering, Christmassy carnival productions and the whole of West German society was present. The director had decided, as usual (and quite rightly too) to have a few extra entertainments for the guests at Prince Orlovsky's party. On this occasion there was to be a piano recital, which inevitably involved the appearance of a piano on the stage. The action of the opera stopped and stage-hands, suitably dressed as flunkeys, brought the piano in on wheels. Perhaps they pushed too hard, perhaps some officious person had over-oiled the ball-bearings to stop them squeaking and confusing the audience with untimely bat-noises, but whatever the cause, the piano became hopelessly out of control on the steeply-raked stage and it ran straight down, gathering speed as it went, and fell into the orchestra pit. Luckily it seems that the players saw it coming and scrambled for safety so the damage was restricted to two flattened tubas and one very dead Bechstein Grand.

INDEX

Index